This Book belongs to an...

Better Basketball

Better Basketball

BRIAN E. COLEMAN

Technical Director
English Basket Ball Association

KAYE & WARD · LONDON
in association with Methuen of Australia
and Hicks Smith, New Zealand

First published by
Kaye & Ward Ltd
21 New Street, London EC2M 4NT
1979

ISBN 0 7182 1462 5

Set in VIP Palatino by S. G. Mason (Chester) Ltd
Printed and bound in Great Britain by Cox & Wyman Ltd
London, Fakenham and Reading

Contents

Acknowledgements

I would like to express my thanks and appreciation to the following people who have helped make this book possible.

Trevor Pountain who took the photographs that appear in this book.

To members of Stockport Belgrade and Padgate College Basketball Clubs and their coach Bill Beswick, for their assistance in the preparation of the demonstration photographs.

Olwen Robinson for typing the manuscript.

Introduction

Basketball is today one of the most popular participant sports in the world. It is played by both men and women, boys and girls, and has achieved its popularity because it is a game of skill rather than strength.

Basketball in its basic concept is a simple game. It is a team passing game, played with the hands, with the object of scoring a goal in a horizontal target (the basket) suspended 10 feet from the floor. The game is played to three basic rules: no contact; no running carrying the ball; and one dribble.

The popularity of Basketball has come from the enjoyment gained in playing a game that involves all players in a fast all action team game. All players are involved in their team's attack and defence. The game demands the individual skills of shooting, dribbling, passing and individual offence and defence, and these when combined with the play of team-mates make basketball a game of all action, that is exhilarating to play.

The author's previous book 'Basketball – techniques, teaching and training' also published by Kaye & Ward, was concerned with teaching and coaching the game. This book is written for the individual player, so that they can learn the correct skills to enable them to play better basketball.

The book is written to assist the individual player to improve his or her skill and is therefore mainly concerned with individual skills and gives only limited coverage to team tactics. Some advice is given on the training that can be carried out when alone or with only a few friends.

The technical terms and jargon used in basketball are explained as the reader progresses through the book.

The successful players perform the simple skills of the game very well. They have achieved their success by dedicated practice having been taught the correct skills as young players. With dedication and through following the advice given in this book, boys and girls can achieve greater success and enjoyment when playing basketball.

Brian E. Coleman

Cup Final Basketball.

The Game

The prime objective of basketball is to score and to score more often than the opposing team. A team will therefore endeavour to gain possession of the ball and through a team combination of their individual skills try to move the ball to a player who is in position on court from where he will have a high percentage chance of scoring with his shot.

Possession of the ball and retaining possession until there is an opportunity of a good shot is important. The moment of change of possession when one team is changing from a defensive to an attacking role should be the first moment to initiate an attack, so as to gain an advantage before the opponents have recovered. This attack, when the team on gaining possession quickly attempts to advance the ball into their *front court* (the half of court containing the basket which the team is attacking) before the defensive team is organised and thus gain position and/or numerical advantage, is called a *fast break*. Each time a team gains possession of the ball they should think of using a fast break.

When the team on attack find they are unable to fast break or, after quickly advancing the ball to the front court, find no opportunity for an early shot, they will need to organise their attack so as to combine individual skills to create a scoring opportunity.

An individual player when on attack has four basic options open to him these are:

> — to shoot
> — to dribble
> — to pass
> — to move

Before he performs any one of these actions he may use a *fake* so as to deceive his opponent as to his intentions.

10

2. Action from a National League gam

Although each player may shoot any time he has the ball on court, his team will be looking for him to take the shot which has a high percentage chance of scoring. The higher percentage shots are those taken closer to the basket, free of opponents' defensive pressure.

Each player will vary in his shooting ability but you should aim as a player to be able to score about 40% of the shots you take within an 18 foot (5.5 m) range of the basket. If you are on attack without the ball you should be endeavouring to get free to receive a pass within this 18 foot range of the basket. Having gained the ball within this range you are now a scoring threat to the defence, especially if upon receipt of the ball you have pivoted to face the basket. Even if you receive the ball just outside this range you should pivot to face the basket so that when you look up at the basket your opponent may be deceived into thinking you are about to shoot and step out to mark you.

The defender who is moving forward away from basket towards the attacking player with the ball is off balance, and as an attacking player in this situation you will look for a chance to dribble aggressively past the opponent towards the basket in an attempt to score from closer to the basket. The aggressive dribble towards the basket is referred to as a *drive*.

If you find, as a player with the ball, you are not in a position to shoot and to dribble the ball is inappropriate, you will need to look for a team-mate who is free to receive your pass.

As a no-contact sport it should in theory be possible in basketball for the team in possession of the ball to retain possession. Basketball is mainly a short passing game, and you should look for a team-mate who is between 10 and 15 feet (3–4.5 m) from you and who is free to receive. Most passes used in the game should be short, sharp and direct to the team-mate.

The receiver of a pass will frequently have had to make some movement to get free of a close marking opponent. This movement should be such that it enables the defender to be momentarily lost, for the receiver to place himself 10 to 15 feet (3–4.5 m) from the team-mate holding the ball and within a range from goal so that when the ball is caught, the player is a potential scoring threat. The new ball handler should now look to shoot or

drive. These may not be possible due to a good recovery by the defender. What do you do now? Obviously look to pass to a team-mate, but which one, you have four to choose from. The first team-mate you should look for is the team-mate who gave you the ball, because he might be moving. In particular he may be cutting towards the basket looking for a return pass. A *cut* is a quick movement made by an attacking player who does not have the ball aiming to gain an advantage over an opposing defender, and usually made towards the basket.

The use of two team-mates working together to create a scoring opportunity is typical of team-plays used in Basketball. A team will arrange its attack to make use of two man and occasionally three man plays. To enable players on the attacking team to work as a team unit they will need some form of organisation. This will be arranged by the team-coach. Through this organisation the team attack will be planned to take maximum advantage of the strengths of individuals on the team and to capitalise on weakness in the opponents' defence.

The position a player will take in his team when on attack will depend upon his own skill, his team-mates' skills and his height compared with his team-mates. Players may roam over the whole playing court, but during most attacks a player will move to one specified position which is identified by the area on court occupied by the player when attacking.

The three basic playing positions are Guard, Forward and Centre and they relate to the position taken when on attack. The diagram shows these areas and the name given to a player who occupies one of the positions. Further information about these positions is given on pages 86 and 87.

For about half the game your team will be on defence. A good team defence is built upon individual defensive ability. This ability includes being able to discourage the good percentage shot, to mark a ball handler, a dribbler or a cutter, and methods to be employed to mark a player who does not have the ball. The defensive team will be endeavouring to gain possession of the ball without conceding a basket. Whereas the attacking player is looking for the high percentage shot, the defenders will try to stop opponents gaining a position for a good shot. The defenders will try to give the

14

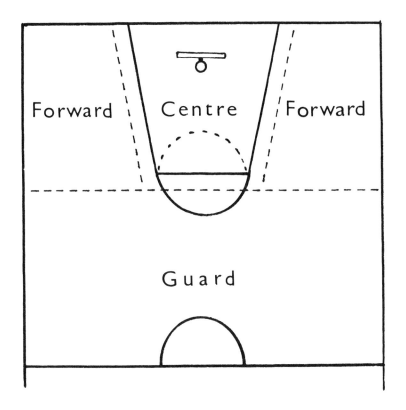

attacking team only the poor percentage shots, these are the long shots and those taken when closely marked.

When the opponents take a low percentage shot the defenders will now attempt to gain the *rebound,* that is retrieve the ball as it rebounds from the ring or backboard after an unsuccessful shot. Once the rebound is gained a new attack can be started initially looking for a fast break.

Shooting

The basic shooting techniques used in the game have the same key points that will help you gain greater success. These points are:

> — Stance and body balance
> — Control of the ball
> — Follow-through
> — Concentration
> — Practice

Stance and body balance

The player taking the shot must be balanced and under control. This is dependent upon the stance and footwork; all successful shots start at the feet. If the shot is taken while on the move then this movement should be towards the basket. If the shot is from a stationary position or taken with a jump, any movement should be up and down on the spot. The stance should be knees slightly flexed with feet apart, one foot slightly ahead of the other. If you are a right handed shooter, you should lead with the right foot, a left handed player will have the left foot slightly ahead to maintain balance. The player when shooting will on most occasions be facing the basket. Figure 4 shows a player with good balance while shooting.

Control of the ball

Shooting a basketball should be thought of as a guiding activity rather than a throw. As a shooter you are trying to guide the ball in the correct direction towards the target. To do this you must control the ball. The ball should be held with both hands so that it is gripped with the pads of the fingers. The fingers are comfortably spread with the shooting hand behind the ball in relation to the basket. The non-shooting hand gives support by gripping

16

4. Shooter showing good balance.　5. Shooter showing good control of the ball.

the ball at the side. The ball is kept close to the body to ensure control and to protect it from defenders. The hands, forearm and elbow should be close to the mid line of the body with the elbow of the shooting hand under the ball, pointing towards the target. The player in figure 5 shows good control of the ball in two hands.

17

6. Shot showing good follow through.

Follow through

All shots start at the feet and the drive up from the feet at the start of the shot continues to the follow-through. The shooter will be holding the ball with the wrist cocked. As the shot is made the arm straightens and the ball is released with a vigorous snap of the wrist and fingers. The shooting arm should follow through, straightening as the ball is flighted towards the

18

7. Shot
showing
good follow
through.

basket. As the target is an 18 inch (45 cm) diameter ring, placed horizontally
at a height of 10 feet (3.05 m) above the ground, you should flight the ball so
it drops down into the basket. Only when taking a shot close to basket, will
you use the backboard. On all other shots aim to give the ball a parabolic
flight path, so that it drops straight into the basket. The players shooting in
figures 6 and 7 show good follow through.

Concentration

To be successful, the shooter must concentrate on the target, throughout the shot. The eyes should be focussed on the target before, during and after the shot. You should not follow the flight of the ball with your eyes. In basketball you do not line the ball and the basket up prior to shooting, rather you guide the ball to basket without looking at the ball. The player shooting in figure 8 shows good balance, and concentration on the target when taking the shot.

Practice

All successful shooters are made through practice. Through practice you build confidence in your ability. You will be more confident if you are on balance; have the ball under control; have developed a good shooting action with arm, wrist and fingers, and have learned to concentrate on the basket. Regular practice is essential if you are to become an accurate shooter. Count the shots you take during practice sessions in 100s rather than 10s. With practice it is possible to guarantee improvement, provided when you practise you use the basic techniques outlined in this book. There are three basic shots used in the game, a lay-up shot, a set shot and a jump shot. These will now be considered in more detail.

Lay-up shot

This is an essential shot for beginners to master and is taken from close to the basket. It is used either by a player who cuts towards the basket, receives a pass on the run and shoots while moving forward towards the basket, or by a player who gathers the ball at the end of a dribble and who shoots on the move without stopping.

In figure 9 the player at the end of a fast break has moved past the defender to take a close to basket shot. The shot is scored by laying the ball on the backboard so that it drops down into the basket. The shooter finds

8. Shooter concentrating on the basket.

9. Lay-up shot.

10d

10e

the appropriate spot on the backboard. For a right handed shooter travelling towards the basket from the right at 45° to the backboard this is a spot in the top right hand corner of the small square marked on the backboard.

Three points to emphasise in the shot are that it is taken on the *run*, with a *jump up* and towards the basket, and with a *reach up* to score.

The player demonstrating the shot in figure 10 is gathering the ball in mid stride at the end of the dribble. He lands first on his right foot, then on his left; taking off from this foot he jumps up towards the basket, releasing the ball from his right hand. Notice that he has his eyes on the target early, that

22

10c   10b   10a

10(a–e) Lay-up shot.

the ball is held in two hands, the high jump being made off the opposite foot to the shooting hand, the reach up to score and the basket being scored off the backboard.

When using this shot from the left hand side of the basket, you should jump off the right foot, using the left hand as the shooting hand. This opposite foot and hand enables you to protect the ball from a defender. This protection of the ball is shown clearly in figure 9. The defender in this situation is likely to cause contact, and therefore foul, in his effort to check the shot.

23

| 11a | 11b | 11c | 11d |

11(a – d) Set shot.

Set shot

This is used when you are shooting from a stationary position. Beginners will find this a useful shot to develop for long shots (15–20 feet) (4.5–6 m) from basket. For experienced players, it is the shooting technique usually used when taking a free throw, and the illustration on this page demonstrates the set shot being used for a free throw. Used in the game the player must get into position and initiate the shot quickly.

24

12. Set shot.   13. Set shot.

    The shot starts with the knees slightly flexed, with the drive from the legs used to give distance to the shot. In figure 11 the player has left the ground as he follows through with the shot. Notice the concentration on the target and the spread of the feet with knees bent, in figure 12 and 13. The player demonstrating in figure 11 shows the release of the ball off the finger tips and the snap of the wrist in the follow-through.

14. Jump shot.

Jump shot

This is the shot most used in the senior game today. The jump shot is a quick shot taken after a vertical jump with the ball being released near the top of the jump. The shot is usually taken at the end of a dribble or after receipt of a pass.

On gathering the ball you establish a balanced position facing the basket, with knees bent and feet spread about shoulder width apart. From this position, you jump upwards, carrying the ball in two hands up past the face to a position in front of the forehead. The ball is held with the shooting hand behind the ball, and the non-shooting supporting the ball at the side. You concentrate on the basket throughout, and having moved the ball past the face you are now looking at the target under the ball as in figure 14. You shoot the ball towards the basket with an extension of the elbow and vigorous wrist and finger action. The timing of the shot should be to jump

26

15. Jump shot.

and then release the ball just prior to peak of your jump.

In figure 15 notice the concentration on the target, the spread of the fingers of the shooting hand behind the ball. The player in this picture has just started his shooting action, the elbow is beginning to extend, and the wrist action that will flight the ball to basket has started. The player is in good body balance and should land on the same spot from where he took off.

A jump shot may be made after a fake to get the defender off balance and so give more space for the shot. A step fake as though to dribble past the defender might be employed and as the defender moves back, the shooter recovers and jumps and shoots. Another move you will need to develop is the use of a jump shot following a short dribble to the side. Remember that when you move into the shot and before the shot is taken, you must be balanced facing the basket.

Shooting practices

When teaching yourself the technique of the basic shots, you should practice shooting from close to the basket. When you are scoring consistently from a close range, then move back. You will then be performing the technique of the shot in a more relaxed manner. Being close to the basket you will be more successful. With success, you will build confidence and to become a good shooter you must have confidence in your own ability.

If you are practising alone start shooting from close to basket. Everytime you score take one pace away from basket and then shoot from the new spot. If you miss take one step closer before shooting. Using this method see how far you can move away from the basket, stepping away from the basket every time you score.

Another good practice if you are working alone is to select spots on the court taking 20 or 25 shots from each spot before moving on. Another similar practice is called 'Golf'. You select several spots on the floor (the 'holes' of the golf course). You then move round the course shooting from each 'hole' until you score. The object is to go round the course in as few shots as possible. This game can be played against an opponent.

Working with a partner you can shoot after receiving a pass. One player is shooting while the other rebounds and passes the ball to the shooter at a new position on the floor. Figure 17 shows two players using this practice. The shooter should take 25 shots before changing with his partner. If the shooter keeps a count of the number scored and his partner counts until the 25 shots have been taken, it is easy to work out the percentage scored by multiplying the total scored by four. You should aim to score 30–40% of your shots.

As your skill develops practice your shots against a defender. A defender who may be making only a limited effort to stop your shot as in figure 16. As you improve your shot, so your partner makes more effort to discourage your shot.

16. Shooting over an opponent.

17. Shooting practice with a partner.

Dribbling

The dribble is used to move with the ball to a new position on court. When used correctly it plays a very important part in attacking basketball, mis-used the dribbler can be a liability to his team. A player with the ball who has not used his dribble is *'alive'*, if you have used your dribble you are *'dead'*. The dribble must be used with purpose. The main uses of the dribble are:

— to penetrate the defence in order to create a scoring opportunity
— to advance the ball into the front court on attack
— to move the ball out of a congested area of the court, thus protecting possession
— to create a passing lane
— to retain possession of the ball in the closing seconds of a game.

The dribble is misused when a player dribbles out of habit or dribbles when it would be better to pass.

You must be able to dribble equally well with either hand, to dribble without looking at the ball, to change direction, and speed, and vary the position of the bouncing ball relative to yourself.

The players in figures 18 and 19 show good dribbling action. Against the defender they protect the ball with their body. The knees and waist are bent. Control of the ball is through a strong wrist and finger action, with the fingers of the dribbling hand, comfortably spread on the top of the ball. Notice that both dribblers have their head up looking where they are going and for the position of other team-mates and opponents.

18 and 19. Dribbler showing good protection and eyes off the ball.

Individual Attack with the Ball

The individual attacking player with the ball is the only player on his team at that moment who can score. His first attacking weapon should be to look for an opportunity to shoot. Therefore the first thing you should do upon receipt of the ball is to look at the basket, not just with your head and eyes, but by pivoting so that you face the basket.

You are now threatening the opposition. If you are within your own scoring range and your opponent has given you space, you can shoot. If

20(a–d) Offensive drive against an opponent who steps forward.

20d

20c

your opponent is close to you, then the option you look to use is a drive (dribble) past the opponent closer to basket. If and when you find yourself a long way from basket out of your scoring range, then an option you may use is a dribble to bring yourself closer to the basket.

It is important to remember that the start of your dribble can be the most important part of the drive. Don't dribble out of habit. Figure 20 (a) shows a player who has just received the ball and pivoted to face the basket. He is now a *triple threat,* he can shoot, drive or pass. With the ball held at the chest he can quickly perform any of these three movements. The defender is uncertain what is going to happen. If he thinks the attacker is about to shoot he may attempt to defend the shot by taking a step closer to the ball handler. As the defender moves his weight forward he is off balance and the attacker can look to drive past the defender. Figure 20 demonstrates this move.

20b   20a

Up and under

For the defender to step forward is only one of a number of mistakes he may make that will give the individual attacking player with the ball a scoring opportunity. We have seen that one mistake the defender can make is an error of balance when he steps forward to defend against a possible shot. This error was created when the attacking player pivoted and faced the basket and with the ball at the chest looked at the basket.

Another useful move for you to develop is sometimes referred to as 'up and under'. This attacking move also involves the defender taking action to mark a possible shot. In this situation the defender jumps up to defend the shot. This move is illustrated in figure 21. The attacking player looks up at the basket at the same time lifting the ball slightly. The defender thinking that a shot is to be made starts to jump to check the shot. The attacking player when making the fake shot keeps his knees bent, and in this position with one foot slightly ahead of the other is in a good position to make a quick start. In the demonstration, the attacking player decides to drive past the leaping defender to the left, he therefore steps past the defender with his right foot and dribbles with his left hand. On any drive past a defender you will aim to step past the defender with one foot and dribble the ball with the opposite hand, thus protecting the ball with the body. The movement of the attacking player is forward, to give added protection, he will also drop the same shoulder as the leading leg, so as to get head and shoulders past the defender. Once you have your head and shoulders past the defender, the greater responsibility for avoiding contact rests with the defender.

21(a–b) Up and und

Step, fake and drive

As an attacking player you can use a fake dribble to force a defender to make an error that will enable you to drive for basket. This move usually involves a step fake in one direction, and then as the defender moves laterally to cover a possible dribble in this direction, the attacking player drives in the new direction. This step fake and drive is demonstrated in figure 22. The attacking player steps to his right with a short step with the right foot. As the defender moves to cover a possible dribble, the attacking player steps again with the right foot only this time, down the left hand side. The attacking player has stepped twice with the right foot using the left foot as the pivot foot.

The rules require that when starting a dribble the ball must be released for the start of the dribble prior to the lifting of the pivot foot.

You may also use a head and shoulder fake to make the defender think you are about to attempt to dribble down one side and as he steps to cover that side, you can drive past on the opposite side.

The step fake and drive, and head and shoulder fake involves the defender *moving* laterally in an effort to mark the attacking player's dribble in a particular direction. If you find when you receive the ball, you are out of shooting range but marked, you can use the dribble to beat the opponent. The simplest way to do this is to start dribbling in one direction and when the defender starts to move to cover, you can change direction, at the same time changing hands, stepping past the defender and protecting the ball with the body, and using the hand away from the defender, for the dribble, as shown in figures 18, 19, 20 and 23.

22(a–b) Step, fake and dri

You should be alert to the defender crossing his legs, when he does this he is in a poor position. figure 23 shows an attacking player going past a defender who has crossed his legs.

Remember that if you are closely marked by a defender with his arms out, as in Figure 24 you can dribble through the arms. The defender must drop his arms otherwise he is responsible for any contact that may result.

23. Drive past a defender who crosses his legs.

24. One versus one.

Dribbling practices

When you are a beginner, you should do a great deal of dribbling practice, practising change of hands, direction and speed, until you can perform equally well with both hands, and without the need to look at the ball. When performing all these dribbling actions, keep crouched, knees bent and head up and ensure that you are bouncing the ball with a wrist action. A useful practice is to perform a zig-zag down the court. Start moving to your right using your right hand, then change direction to move to your left using your left hand, and then to the right, changing direction every 15 feet (4.5 m) covered.

As you increase in dribbling ability you should work against an opponent, trying some of the moves covered earlier. Initially when working against an opponent have them co-operate with you by making the mistake you require.

You are developing your dribbling to use against an opponent, so that you can take advantage of mistakes they may make. What are the mistakes you are looking for? The first mistake is that of not being in position, between the attacking player with the ball and the basket. The other mistakes are those of balance, balance relative to the attacking player and the basket, these are:

(a) Moving towards the attacking player (see page 32)
(b) Jumping up to check an anticipated shot (see page 34)
(c) Moving laterally — right or left (see page 36)
(d) Moving backwards towards the basket and giving time for a shot.

Passing

Basketball is a team game and your team is able to move the ball to a scoring position on the court through good passing. The skills of shooting and dribbling may be the spectacular skills of the game, but the success of your team will depend upon sound passing. Basketball is a game of possession of the ball and because it is difficult to practise passing when working alone it is often a neglected skill. Your team will not only be endeavouring to retain possession of the ball but also to move the ball to a player who is in a position for a good shot. Safety and effectiveness in passing the ball must be stressed. The ball should not only be safely passed but it must also be received by the receiver when he wants the ball and where he wants the ball. It is a poor pass if a team-mate has moved free and then does not receive the ball until the defender has recovered, equally it is a poor pass if the player who is free receives the ball near his feet rather than at the position from which he can either shoot or pass the ball on quickly to a team-mate. Good passing can lead to good shooting.

The ball should be held firmly with the fingers of both hands, so that thumbs are behind and the fingers along the side of the ball. The ball should be held in the area from in front of the chest up to a position above head height. With the ball held thus the ball handler has his head up and can see what is going on around him on court. Figures 25 and 26 show the same player holding the ball in each of these two positions. The ball handler can now more successfully time his pass. Remember basketball is a short passing game – 10 to 15 feet (3–4.5 m) is a good passing range and passes should be sharp, crisp and accurate. The ball should be released quickly at an appropriate speed so that the team-mate will have no difficulty catching the ball. If the ball travels too fast the receiver may have difficulty in catching it, if it goes too slow then defenders will have time to move and intercept. Remember that the defenders will have more time to move and

25. Player with the ball in position ready to make a chest pass.

26. Player with the ball in position ready to make an overhead pass.

intercept the longer the pass. You will endeavour to deceive your opponents so that the interception is more difficult. Disguising passing intentions can be achieved through the use of fakes and feints prior to passing, but equally effective disguising of intentions can be achieved by not staring at the team-mate, using peripheral vision to see the team-mate. Eliminate any wind-up to your passes aiming to release the ball quickly through the use of a vigorous wrist and finger action.

Chest pass

The player in figure 31 is about to pass the ball to a team-mate who has moved free of a defender to receive the ball. Notice the hand being held up by the potential receiver to indicate to his team-mate where he wants the ball. Two players are involved in a successful pass, the passer and the receiver. The receiver helps his team-mate by moving free to create a passing lane and signalling for the ball. The most appropriate pass for the ball handler to use in Figure 31 is a *chest pass,* this is a short range two-hand pass made from in front of the chest to a team-mate who is free from an opponent. The ball is passed directly to the team-mate by extending the arms, wrists and fingers in the direction of the intended. The arms follow through fully in the direction of the pass. The players in figure 27a are demonstrating this pass. The passer as she makes the passes steps forward slightly in the direction of the pass, note the position of the hands on the ball and full follow through as the pass is made to the team-mate who catches the ball in two hands ready for the immediate return pass.

27 (a–b) Chest pas

28 (a–b) Overhead pass.   28a

Overhead pass

Another basic pass that all players need to master is the two hand overhead pass. Figure 26 shows the pass about to be used in a game by England Guard, Dave Shelley. Here he is about to pass the ball to a team-mate moving out to receive the ball. The passing lane created by holding the ball high enables a quick direct pass to be made to the team-mate. The overhead pass is a useful skill to develop for use when playing against a smaller opponent or when closely marked. In the demonstration in Figure 28 (a) the passer is holding the ball in two hands overhead with the arms slightly flexed. The ball is passed with a vigorous snap of the wrist and fingers, making as little use of a wind-up of the arms as possible. Notice that in figure 28 (b) the follow through of the wrist and finger with the arms still held high.

44

28b

Other passes

In the demonstration of the overhead pass the passer is passing through the gap over the defender's head between the arms. Another gap exists under the outstretched arms of the defender. When passing under the arms of a defender it is usual to bounce the ball. The use of a *bounce pass* is useful against a tall opponent. The action of a two-hand bounce pass is similar to the chest pass except the ball starts at a lower level, i.e. at waist or hip level, and the ball travels to the team-mate via the floor. When using this pass think of skidding the ball to a team-mate rather than bouncing. The disadvantage of this pass is that it is slower and therefore slightly easier for the defender to intercept. As you become more proficient as a passer so you can develop the type and range of passes you can use. It will be improtant to develop a passing action that makes use of a vigorous snap of the wrist and

29. One hand pass.

fingers. If you develop a strong wrist action you will be able to use *one hand passes.* Even with one hand passes remember you need accuracy, correct passing lane to the team-mate, deception and appropriate speed so that the defender does not have time to move into a position to intercept. Figure 29 shows a player in a poor position, closely marked, off balance with his feet off the ground. He has obviously jumped to prevent a ball going out-of-bounds. To make a successful pass to a team-mate he will need to use a vigorous snap of the wrist and fingers to flight the ball quickly and accurately. This skill will only have been developed through practice.

46

Passing practices

A good passing practice to use when working alone is to pass against a wall as in figure 30. You can place a target on the wall and practise passing at the target. Try using a variety of passes, working with one as well as both hands. Throughout these practices stress the use of wrist and fingers.

With a partner you can extend the type of passes you have to make. All the passes demonstrated have been made from a stationary position. To become a good passer you must be able to pass on the move. This you can practise with the partner, stressing taking the ball on the run.

With a third player a good practice is pig in the middle (see figure 28). You are now making your passes against a defender and will need to react and vary your passes according to his position and stance.

30. Passing practice.

Pass reception

When moving free when you have not the ball your aim is to create a passing lane for the team-mate who is holding the ball. You help your team-mate by giving him a clear signal with one or both hands, to indicate where you want to receive the ball. Your signal not only indicates your readiness to the passer but also prepare yourself to make the catch. In figure 31 the player in white No. 6 is signalling with his left hand to indicate where he wants to receive the ball. This you will notice is on the side of the player away from the defender.

31. Pass reception.

Catching

Passing and catching are closely related skills. When you catch the ball your technique of receiving should place the ball in a position ready to shoot, drive or pass. Therefore use two hands to make the catch cushioning the ball with the fingers keeping the palms of the hands off the ball. If the ball slaps into the palm of your hand it is a poor catch.

To make a clean catch concentrate on the ball, so that you can ascertain the flight of the ball correctly, in particular concentrate on the early flight of the ball just after it leaves the passer's hands. Having ascertained the flight of the ball adjust your position so as to get as near as possible behind the line of flight and step to meet the ball. This movement to meet the ball makes it more difficult for a defender to step in front of the receiver and gain an interception. Having made early contact on the ball with both hands, the receiver should bring the ball under control by relaxing the elbows and bringing the ball to a triple threat position ready for the next movement.

The catch will of course be helped if an accurate pass of the appropriate speed is made. The receiver will find it easier to catch the ball if it is not spinning and/or travelling too fast.

Protection of the ball

When catching the ball in two hands and holding it in a position in front of the upper body, the player is now in a strong position. He should have his head up able to see close marking opponents. To give the ball more protection, a closely marked player, on catching the ball can turn his grip so that one hand is on top and the other underneath the ball. This makes it more difficult for an opponent to knock the ball away.

Additional protection is given by the use of a pivot away from the defender. In figure 31 the ball handler has pivoted and is holding the ball away from the defender. Note that he is still looking forwards towards the basket so as to be ready for a quick pass to a team-mate who is free closer to basket.

32. Protecting the ball against a close marking defender.

33. Protection of the ball when dribbling.

It is important that the player does not over protect. The dribbler when going past an opponent uses the hand away from the defender, but does not place the ball so that the ball is bounced beside his hip, this would slow his progress. Figure 32 shows good protection of the ball on a dribble that still permits an attacking movement forward.

Moving free to receive a pass

A player who wishes to get free to receive a pass will have to make one or a combination of the following movements to lose the opponent.

1. Move towards the ball.
2. Move away from the ball and then move back to receive the ball in the space created by the movement away from the ball.
3. Move towards the basket and then go back out to receive.
4. Use of a change of direction and change of speed.

In figure 34 the player in the dark vest waiting to receive, initially steps away from the ball and then he moves back to receive. In this demonstration the move is being used to bring the ball into play after the opponents have scored. Notice that the receiver is signalling with both hands and when catching the ball in both hands he will be protecting the ball with his body.

An important method of getting free to receive a pass is step towards the basket and then move out to receive. In figure 35 (a) the defender marking the potential receiver is marking the possible passing lane by moving slightly to one side of the attacking player and putting a hand up and in the direct passing lane. This is called *overplaying*. To get free the attacking player steps to basket, then changes direction and moves back out to receive. When he uses this change of direction he will also use a change of speed, making the initial movement to basket at walking pace and then running as he moves out to receive. The receiver should of course be endeavouring to get a free at a spot on court where he will be a scoring threat, that is within 21 feet (6.40 m) of basket, and at a good passing range from the team-mate, that is with the 10 to 15 feet (3–4.5 m) range.

On page 86 an offensive manoeuvre called Give and Go is shown. This move involves the use of a change of direction and speed by an attacking player to get free to receive a pass. The move involves two attacking players, one player passes to a team-mate and then steps away from the direction of the pass, makes a quick change of direction and cuts past the defender for basket looking for a return from his team-mate.

34(a–b) Getting free to receive a pass by
moving to the ball.

35(a–c) Getting free to receive a pass by stepping towards the basket and then moving out.

Body control and footwork

To be a good shooter, dribbler, passer, defender, or rebounding, you must have good body control. The player in figure 36 has proper balance and good body control. He has achieved this by establishing a good stance with feet apart spread approximately shoulder width apart, with the knees bent. The head is up and over the base established by the feet. The weight is evenly distributed over the feet which are flat on the floor.

36. Body balance.

37. Quick start.

A quick start will be helped through the spread of the feet, and the low centre of gravity with the knees bent. Movement of one foot now creates imbalance and a drive from this foot enables the quick start to be made. Figure 37 shows a dribbler making a quick start. Note the low position that should enable him to 'sprint' past the defender on a straight drive for basket.

Stopping

The basketball player needs to be able to stop when he takes the ball at the end of a dribble or from a pass. In doing this he is limited by the rules. The basis of the rules is the use of a two count rhythm when coming to a stop and the *pivot*. A pivot according to the rules occurs 'when a player who is holding the ball steps once or more than once in any direction with the same foot, the other foot called the pivot foot being kept at its point of contact with the floor'. The pivot foot having been established, it cannot be changed, nor may it be lifted and grounded again with the ball still in the player's possession. It may be lifted when you shoot or pass. The pivot is used to change your position when you are holding the ball.

Figure 38 shows a player using a two count rhythm to come to a stop with the ball. The player catches the ball in the air and lands first on the right foot (count one) and then steps on the left foot (count two) as he stops. Notice the lowering of the weight to establish balance. The player in this stopping action can only use his right foot (count one foot) as his pivot foot. This method of stopping is called a *stride stop*.

A player can use a one-count rhythm in coming to a stop with the ball. This is demonstrated in figure 39. The player taking the ball in the air lands on both feet simultaneously. His feet are well spread and he bends his knees, maybe too much in figure 39 (c), to maintain his balance. Having caught the ball in the air and landed two feet simultaneously, the player may select either foot as the pivot foot depending on the situation in the game. The method of stopping is called a *jump stop*.

The same rule regarding selection of the pivot foot also applies if the ball is caught with both feet on the ground. In figure 39 because the defender is off line not between opponent and basket, the attacking player should pivot on this left foot stepping back towards basket with his right foot. If the defender had been off line on the other side, the right foot would have been used as the pivot foot.

Body balance and footwork practices

Whenever you are practising maintain good balance by keeping your knees bent, feet spread and flat on the floor.

With a partner to pass you the ball you can practise the stride and the jump stops demonstrated in figures 38 and 39. Make sure when practising the stride stop, that you practise landing using either foot as the one count

38(a–c) Stride stop.

39(a–c) Jump stop.

foot. That is land left-right as well as right-left as you stop.

Working alone you can practise using the two stops to pick up the ball at the end of a dribble. Figure 40 shows a player having used a jump stop to pick the ball up at the end of a dribble.

To help you use the pivot correctly work close to the basket with a partner who will act as a defender. Use a jump stop as you receive a pass from your partner, now try different pivots to step past the opponent, so as to create space for a shot.

Due to its greater flexibility, more emphasis should be given to develop the use of the jump stop.

40. A jump stop used to complete a dribble.

Individual Defence

The basic defence used in the game is man to man defence, where each individual defender is responsible for marking one opponent. Each defender is assigned one opponent to mark, and they stay defending against that opponent throughout their time on court. You will usually be assigned to mark an opponent who is a similar height, speed and skill to yourself.

To be an effective defender and able to play your part within your team's defence you need to be aware of your aim. To help you understand your role as a defender we will consider the defending of the high percentage scoring area under two headings; defending the ball and defending the man in relation to the danger area. When defending the ball your team will aim to prevent shots being taken in the danger area; prevent passes being made into the area; and prevent opponents from dribbling the ball into the danger area. This will then leave the opponents with only the low percentage scoring chances!

Your defence against a man in relation to the high percentage scoring area will be to prevent him receiving a pass in the danger area (a player without the ball cannot score); and to prevent the opponent gaining a rebound following a missed shot.

Basic defensive stance

Your basic defensive position is directly in line between the opponent and the basket you are defending. Taking this position you can prevent the attacking player from taking the most direct and quickest route to basket. The attacking player can move around the court freely, so as a defender you will need to adopt a stance that will permit you to make constant adjustments of position. The recommended defensive stance is shown in Figures 41 and 42. The defender is facing the opponent, with the feet flat on the

41 and 42. Defensive stance.

floor and spread about shoulder width apart, one foot slightly in advance of the other. The knees are bent, hips flexed and head up. The eyes are focussed on the opponent, a useful place to centre your attention is on their waist. This stance permits the defender to make rapid movements in any direction. The defender in following the opponent tries to use a sliding action of the feet, aiming to keep the centre of gravity low by bending the knees. With this stance and method of moving the defender should be able to make quick changes of position in order to maintain the position between opponent and the basket. The use of the feet to move play a vital part in defending. The defender's arms are up with the elbows flexed and the hands held at between waist and head height with the palms of the hand facing the opponent.

60

Defending against the ball handler

Regardless of the team defensive tactic that your coach may decide to use the attacking player holding the ball must always be marked. Exactly how you play against the ball handler can vary with your team defensive tactic but whatever tactics are employed you must be prepared to think. You should concentrate on the opponent and try to work out what he is likely to do next, relating your thinking to the defensive aims given earlier and the offensive options open to the opponent. How far is the opponent from the basket? Has he dribbled? Can he dribble equally well with either hand? The latter is unlikely, so as a defender you may move slightly *off-line*, that is take up a position slightly to one side of your opponent to mark his strong dribbling hand, but still remaining between opponent and the basket.

Thinking on defence is the second most important aspect of good defence. In figure 43 the defender has moved close to the attacking player with the ball and put his hands up so as to discourage the shot or the pass to the under basket area, he can do this safely because the attacking player has already used his dribble and is 'dead' i.e. has no dribble to come. Good defenders use their feet and their brains to defend well.

43. Defence against a ball handler.

Defending against the shooter

An attacking player you think is about to shoot should not be allowed an unrestricted shot. A defender can discourage or distract the shooter by raising one or both hands so as to break the shooter's concentration on the basket as in figure 44. With the hands up the shooter might worry that the defender is going to check the shot. Figure 45 shows two defenders putting the shooter under a great deal of pressure. If the shooter is very close to the defender, the defender's hand should be above his head. Fouls on the shooter occur because of incorrect use of the hands by the defender. For example an attempt to check the shot could lead to contact being made with

44. Defence against a shooter.

45. Defence against a shoote

the shooter's hand – a personal foul. Figure 46 shows good hand position by defender number 11 against a close opponent who is shooting. His team-mate number 6 is at fault and is likely to foul the shooter with his right hand. It takes exceptional skill to be able to make the kind of defensive check shown in Figure 47, and it is better not to try to check the shot.

When defending against a shooter you should look for clues that indicate

47. Defensive check against a shot.

the opponent is about to shoot. Has he a particular shooting style? Does he make preliminary movements prior to his shot? Has the attacking player a favourite shooting spot on court?

Against a shooter you must ensure that all shots are taken under pressure, this pressure is obtained by being close to the opponent and make good use of the hands and arms to distract the shooter without committing a foul.

65

Defending against the dribbler

Under this heading we will consider defending against the opponent who is about to start a dribble as well as defending against the opponent who is already dribbling. First we should go back to thinking on defence. Has the opponent you are marking a favourite dribbling hand? Does he use particular fakes? Has he favourite moves? It is likely that your opponent will favour one hand and you must quickly work out which hand he favours, so you can mark him slightly off line. If he is right handed you would move slightly off line to your left (the dribbler's right). In this position you should have your left foot forward, so you are encouraging the dribbler to move to his left, your right. With your left foot forward you are ready to move to the right, and the dribbler will be forced to use his weaker hand or if he does decide to continue to use only his right hand to dribble the ball it will be difficult for him to protect the ball with his body.

When the attacking player starts to dribble you must get your feet moving so as to maintain your position leading the dribbler, see figures 48 and 49. Your initial reaction should be to shift back slightly towards the basket and away from the dribbler. Having moved away from the dribbler you now shift you position to keep between opponent and the basket. You will recall from page 36 that a method of beating a defender using a dribble was to fake to dribble one side by using a foot fake and then as the defender moved laterally to cover to change and move down the other side. It is the lateral movement that beats the defender, when you are defending make the shift backwards your first movement so you have space to recover if the opponent is attempting a foot fake and drive.

When marking a dribbler keep you hands down, using your hands and arms to assist your balance and to discourage the dribble. Try to keep your palms facing the ball so that if a chance presents itself you can deflect the ball from the dribbler. Beware of committing a foul when trying to steal the ball, you should be using your feet so that the dribbler's only direct route to basket is one through the middle of your chest which would be a foul by the dribbler. In figure 50 the defender has held a good position against the dribbler who is charging in to defender and therefore committing the foul.

48 and 49. Defence against a dribbler.

50. Defence against a dribbler.

Defending against an opponent without the ball

This aspect of individual defence can be considered for three situations in the game: marking an opponent away from the ball; marking an opponent cutting to basket; and marking an opponent playing centre position in their attack.

When marking the opponent away from the ball you need to make a change to your stance and position on court. You should alter your stance so you can see both your opponent and the ball. Your opponent is not going to score so you can also move away from your opponent closer to the basket. This step back towards the basket is called *'sagging.'* The further your opponent is from the ball the further you will be from him as the defender, a useful guide is that you should be one pace away from him for

51. Man to man defence.

every pass he is from the ball. In figure 51 you will see that the defender under the basket is two paces away from the attacking player number 6. This attacking player is two passes from the ball.

Even if your opponent is some way from the basket you should not take your eyes off him, if you do he may cut to a new position and you will be beaten. The more difficult cutter you will have to mark is the attacking player who has just passed the ball and who cuts to basket looking for the return pass. You should react to this player in the same way as you react to a player starting a dribble: that is, as he passes the ball step back. This gives you time and space to cover a possible fake and cut. When marking a cutter aim to keep ahead of him and try to get to the spot he is heading for first. You should keep your arms up in an effort to discourage passes to the cutter.

The opponent centre will usually be the tallest player in their team and if he receives a pass close to basket, the defence will find it very difficult to prevent the shot, so instead you try to prevent him receiving a pass by adjusting your defensive position so you can put your hand in the direct passing lane from the ball handler to the centre. Figure 52 shows the defender marking the opposing centre number 10. He has moved his position to the side of the centre and has a hand up and in the passing lane. In figure 51 the defender marking the centre, number 11, has help from a team-mate who has moved away from his opponent (sagged) who is a long way from basket and unlikely to score even if he did receive the ball.

Blocking out and rebounding

An opportunity for a shot will depend initially on the team having possession of the ball. While the opponents have the ball it is not possible for your team to score, so you must make every effort to gain possession of the ball in any 'free ball' situations. The majority of free ball situations occur after a shot has been taken and missed. Both teams will be out to gain the new possession of the ball through blocking-out and rebounding.

Blocking-out is the positioning of a player in relation to an opponent so as to prevent the opponent from being able to move to basket and gain the rebound. For the defender who has maintained a position between his opponent and the basket it should be relatively easy to gain a position that will block the attacking player from the inside position close to the backboard. When the shot goes up your first reaction should be to watch your opponent to see which way he moves. You then pivot into his path so as to face the backboard with the opponent behind you. Attacking player will be trying to block-out defender and in figure 53 the player in white number 9 has gained an inside position against the opponent number 10 as his team-mate shoots.

52. Defending to prevent pass reception.
53. Blocking out.

54. Tip-in
shot.

If the attacking players gain the inside position they may be able to
attempt to tip the ball straight back into the basket as in figure 54, or to land
and then look for an opportunity to go straight back for the shot as in figure
55.

55. Offensive player looks for a shot following a rebou

56. Rebound.

Rebounding is the term used to describe the actual jumping to retrieve the ball as it rebounds from the ring or backboard after a missed shot. Having gained the inside position and blocked your opponent from the ball you should time your jump so as to jump up and slightly forward, lifting the arms vigorously to grasp in the ball in two hands as the player is doing in figure 56. To gain maximum height to your rebounding start the jump from

74

a wide base, with feet flat on the floor, knees bent and arms held about shoulder height. Having gained the rebound do not bring the ball in close to the body. Keep the ball away from the body, positioning it away from the opponent as in figure 56.

Practices of individual defence and rebounding

The practices you can use to improve your individual defence, should be carried out against an opponent. One versus one and two versus two games provide excellent opportunity not only for attacking players to improve their skill but also for the defenders. Because good footwork is such an important part of good individual defence you should do some practices that focus attention on footwork. A good practice is one versus one against an opponent only the defender keeps his hands behind his back and the ball handler tries to dribble past, the defender can only use his feet to maintain good position. Another useful defensive practice is to move defensively against a dribbler who is doing the zig zag practice (see page 39).

Working alone you can improve your defensive footwork by doing the zig zag practice as though you are marking an opponent. Take a good defensive position, knees bent feet flat on the floor shoulder width apart, from this position shuffle your feet as though you were maintaining a defensive position against a dribbler who every so often changes direction. Do this zig zag movement down the court.

Rebounding is a matter of improving your jumping ability and timing. Repetition jumps to touch the backboard is a good exercise, starting from a position with knees bent and arms down jump to reach and touch the backboard. See how many times you can touch the backboard in 30 seconds. To improve your timing practise tipping the ball against the backboard. Try first to make 10 consecutive tips against the backboard, and then try to increase the number. Use alternate hands and practise working from both sides of the backboard.

Fast Break

The fast break is an attractive style of attack to watch and great fun to play. It is the quickly developed attack that involves running by all members of the team with quick movement of the ball trying to get one player free so that he can take an easy shot clear of all defenders. In figures 57 and 58 the fast break is being finished with a player taking a lay-up shot. Because movements are made quickly down court it makes demands on the skill of players to be able to do the simple things well that is to catch, pass, dribble and shoot, and to do them quickly and efficiently. Time is important, any time wasted will lead to the breakdown in the fast break. The good fast break is quick, but controlled.

The fast break is the first attack that should be attempted by the attacking team. The attack starts immediately the team gains possession of the ball, which could be from an interception or more likely from gaining a rebound. The simplest fast break is for one player on the attacking team to break down court and have the ball thrown to him while he is alone. However the opponents are unlikely to allow a team to use this type of fast break through the game and there is always a danger that the breaking player goes too early and leaves his team-mates defending four against five.

What will be needed is a fast break that involves all members of the new attacking team working as a team unit to gain a numerical advantage by changing quickly from defence to attack on the change of possession. In considering the fast break three phases can be studied: the gaining possession and the outlet pass; the middle phase taking the ball down court; and the final phase leading to the shot.

Gaining possession and the outlet pass

Possession of the ball to start a fast break will usually be made by gaining a rebound. A fast break can also be started following an interception, when

57 and 58. Scoring at the end of a fast break.

the break is started in this manner the teams move quickly to the second phase of the break. First the ball must be moved away from the opponents or the congested area under the basket. This will usually be achieved by passing the ball to the side of the court. In figure 59 player number 10 having gained the rebound is quickly passing the ball to the side of the court. In figure 60 the new attack is being started by the player in possession looking for a team-mate who is breaking quickly down court.

In the demonstration illustrated in figure 61 the fast break is being started from a rebound from a missed shot. The rebounder number 7 takes the ball

77

59. Outlet pass to start a fast break.

60. Player looks for an outlet pass to start a fast break.

in two hands. He lands and looks for an outlet pass to a team-mate at the side of the court. Number 10 who can be seen in figure 61 (a) blocking his opponent out as the rebound is collected, breaks out to the side of the court approximately opposite the free throw line. In this position he is able to receive the quick pass out from the rebounder. By taking the ball to the side the initial movement of the attack is away from the area of the court that will be congested, that is the under basket area. The rebounder taking the ball on the left hand side of the backboard makes his outlet pass to the same side of court.

78

61(a–b) Rebound and outlet pass to start a fast break.

Middle phase of the fast break — filling the lanes

Having moved the ball from the congestion of the under basket area the attacking team must now move the ball down court quickly. They aim to move the ball down court and gain a numerical advantage before the opponents have recovered and organised their defence. To do this the attacking team endeavours to fill three attacking lanes as they move the ball down court. In the demonstrated fast break in figure 62 *(a)* the player who was furthest away from the rebound situation, who did not receive the outlet pass, breaks down the middle of the court to receive a pass from the player who caught the outlet pass. This player number 5 takes the ball on the move, dribbles past the defender and leads the break down court. The player leading the attack must not be left alone. Other team-mates should strive to get in on the fast break. As they move down court, they should spread out so that the fast breaking team have two players occupying the lanes alongside the player with the ball. These lanes are 10–15 feet apart – one lane goes down the middle and one down each side of the court. In figure 62 *(b)* the attacking team have filled the three lanes with the ball being dribbled down the court in the middle lane. There is a danger that the attacking team tries to move the ball down court too fast and lose control.

Final phase of the fast break

The attacking team must appreciate that they are trying to outnumber the opponents and create the first good shot. To be able to use a fast break successfully all members of the team should be striving to get on the break. In the demonstrated fast break the attacking team has clearly gained a numerical advantage and it can be expected that the dribbler in the middle lane will drive straight to basket for a shot. In the game the opponents may be able to move players back on defence. The fast breaking team will obviously still be trying to get a lay-up shot, but if this is not possible they

80

62(a–b) Middle phase of a fast break.

63. Final phase of a fast break showing defence.

will be looking for an opportunity to take an uninterrupted 10 to 15 feet (3–4.5 m) shot. With defender back in position the fast breaking team should present them with a 'problem' by attacking the basket and so commit one defender. The attacking team should aim to keep spread out and make as few passes as possible. The player with the ball should drive for basket and only pass off when stopped. Any passes that are made should be crisp and made to the team-mate so that he can easily handle the ball and not lose his forward momentum.

In figure 63 the attacking team have three players against two defenders and this should lead to a scoring opportunity. Player number 5 dribbling the ball down the middle has committed one defender, he should now quickly pass off so that his team-mates are two versus one against the defender under the basket. Player number 5 having passed off should stop at the free throw line and not move in under the basket and cause congestion that will be to the advantage of the defenders.

Defending against a fast break

The attacking team is aiming to gain a numerical advantage and to do this they will try to start their attack immediately they gain possession of the ball. The simple things to do to prevent your opponents outnumbering you are to defensively fast break and to delay the start of the fast break. The defensive fast break demands that players respond instantly to the change in possession. With the opponents more likely to be trying to start the fast break after gaining a rebound, the player who has rebounded the ball should be marked, so that he will be more concerned with protecting the ball than throwing a quick outlet pass.

Should the attacking team gain a numerical advantage as in figure 63 the defenders must still know how to play so as to prevent the easy shot. The defenders in this figure are already in the correct position, one behind the other in tandem formation. The front defender is correctly marking the ball. Should the middle attacking player pass off to one of the cutters moving down the side, then the defender under the basket should move out to take the ball, and the front defender now drops back to cover the under basket area. If both defenders keep their arms up they can make the cross court pass very difficult for the opposition to make. The defenders want the attacking team to make one more pass, each pass uses up more time, time for other defenders to move back into their defensive positions.

Practices for the fast break

The fast break is a team activity so it is difficult to undertake individual practices. If you have a partner to work with you can practise your running down court passing the ball backwards and forwards between you, scoring each end of court. When passing on the move it is important to learn to use a natural running action with no hops, skips or bounds. Passes should be made with two hands and the ball passed in front of the team-mate so that he runs on to the ball.

With three players a good practice is two versus one, played the full length of court. The three players start at one end of the court with the player who is to defend standing at the free throw line. The two attacking players stand under the backboard, one of them lobs the ball onto the backboard for his team-mate to jump and rebound. Once the ball has been caught by the rebounder the defender can move. The two players on attack endeavour to beat the defender down to the other end of court and score. This is good practice for the attacking players to learn to commit the defender by driving straight at the basket and then pass off to the team-mate quickly and safely. The attacking player without the ball must move so that he keeps spread out and gives his team-mate an easy pass.

Team Attack

It is not the intention of this book to cover team play in detail. The attacking team will aim to turn each possession of the ball into a scored basket. To be able to do this they must combine their individual skill to move the ball to a position on court for a shot that will have a high percentage chance of being scored. Most team plays on attack are created through individual players working alone or with two players combining to create a scoring opportunity for one of the pair. In the next pages two basic two versus two attacking plays the 'give and go' and a 'screen' will be briefly covered.

To be able to make use of these individual and team attacking skills there must be some organisation of the attacking team. This organisation should be such that when on attack each attacking player is a threat to the basket. If he has the ball in his possession he should be facing the basket, if he is without the ball he should be at a distance from the basket where he did receive the ball he would be a threat to the opposition.

To be able to create scoring opportunities involves movement of the ball and/or of players. Movement creates problems for the defenders who should react to each movement. The attacking team is trying to move the ball to the high percentage scoring area. However they cannot have all their players in the highest percentage scoring area, instead they will spread out, usually about 10 to 15 feet (3–4.5 m) apart, so they can easily make passes to team-mates. This spreading out gives support to the ball handler and usually aims to keep the under basket area relatively free. The spreading out through creating space between team-mates gives room for them to execute scoring plays that involve drives or cuts to basket.

Usually the attacking team will organise itself into a particular formation, they vary according to the number of players they have in the different playing positions, forward, centre and guard. A common formation is called a 2.1.2. attack. In this the team has two players in the Guard position,

85

64. 2.1.2. Attacking formation.

one playing at Centre and the other two in the Forward position. A 2.1.2. attack is shown in figure 64.

A player in the *guard* position will play facing the basket working from the area of the court from the free-throw line back towards the half-way line. They are usually the shorter players on the team and will need to be good ball handlers and capable drivers. Frequently a more experienced player will be in the guard position so he can direct the team's plays.

The player who plays *forward* plays facing the basket in the area of the court from the free throw line to the end line, that is at the side of the court. A forward is usually one of the taller players in the team. They must have good drive and shot from the side of the court and they must be prepared to move in to obtain rebounds. The *centre* will be the tallest member of the team and will play close to the basket so as to take advantage of his height. They play around the restricted area and must be good rebounders and capable close to basket shooters.

Give and go

This is a two player attacking move in which one player passes to a team-mate and then cuts towards basket looking for a return pass.

In the demonstration in figure 65 it is being executed between a guard and a forward on the right hand side of the court. The ball has been passed from the guard, number 10, to his team-mate who has moved free. The guard having passed starts to move away from the ball. His opponent starts to move laterally to stay with the guard. The attacking player now executes a quick change of direction and now cuts inside the moving defender. The forward who is looking towards the basket has no difficulty passing the ball to the cutter. When you are playing in the game you should always be on the lookout for an opportunity to cut for basket after making a pass to a team-mate. When playing against an inexperienced defender you may find that when you make a pass from the guard position to a forward who is ahead of you that your opponent turns his head to look at the ball. At this moment you are unmarked and should immediately cut for basket.

When you are using the give and go it is better to execute the cut on the side of your defender where the ball is being held. If you beat your opponent with your cut you will now have a two versus one situation against your team-mate's defender. This has been created in the demonstration in figure 65.

65(a–c) Give and Go.

a

Screen play

A screen is a term used to describe a legal position taken up by a player who obstructs the movement of an opponent. A screen aims to impede the progress of a defender momentarily and to allow an attacking player to move free. In the photographs in figures 66 and 67, taken from games, the

66. A screen by player No. 11 about to be used by the dribbler.

b   c

player with the ball is trying to move on the dribble so that their defender is unable to follow them due to the position taken up by the team-mate. The team-mate in both instances is standing on the piece of floor that the defender will want to go across to be able to stay in the best defensive position.

67. A screen by player No. 12 being used by the dribbler.

68(a–c) Screen play.

a

A screen play is demonstrated in figure 68 being used by two players in the guard position. The ball is passed from one of the guards to the other. The new ball handler pivots and faces the basket looking for an opportunity to drive to basket. His opponent has a good defensive position. To beat this opponent the ball handler's team-mate moves to take a position close to the defender so that the drive can be made to basket. You can see in figure 68 *(c)* that the defender's progress is impeded due to the position of the screen.

It is important that the player setting the screen is stationary when he is used, otherwise he will be guilty of a foul.

Using the basic principle of the screen it is possible to vary the way the attacking team uses this play. A screen play can be created where the screen is set for a team-mate who does not have the ball. In the demonstration in figure 68 for example the ball could have been held by a player at right forward. Number 6 would have still set the screen in the same fashion only this time his team-mate would have cut not driven for basket.

You will have noticed in the give and go and the screen play that the attacking player moving free moves to the under basket area. It is important

90

b   c

for the attacking team to keep this area of court relatively free of players. The defensive team will try to keep defenders in this area.

Practice of give and go and screen plays

The best and most popular practice for these team skills is to play two versus two. This practice game is played into one basket, with the attacking pair trying to score. They continue to attack until they score or lose possession. To create a new attacking situation the new attacking team bring the ball to half court and start their attack towards the same basket. While they are moving the ball to the half way line the previous attacking team take up their defensive positions.

In figure 69 four players are playing two versus two. If the attacking player number 11 cuts close to the right of his team-mate he may lose his defender, whose progress may be impeded by the screening situation created by the ball handler. As number 11 cuts for basket close to his team-mate he should expect a short range pass.

69. Two versus two.

Team Defence

The ability of a team to play as a team unit on defence will depend a great deal upon their individual defensive ability. The defending team will endeavour to match the attacking team's ability with defensive ability. Fast players will be marked by fast players, tall attacking players will be marked by the tallest defenders. The deployment of defenders will aim to have the tallest players close to backboard so that they are in a position to gain defensive rebounds.

The defending team will be trying to adequately defend the high percentage scoring area. This has been covered on page 59. It should be noted that the defensive team will aim to put their defensive pressure towards the ball, making sure that the ball is always marked, that potential receivers are marked and that passing lanes into the high percentage scoring area are covered. The defending team will try to have depth to their defence, so that if an opponent moves free under the basket he can be picked up and marked so that no opponent has an easy shot.

Finally one important aspect to team defence that has not been mentioned so far is communication. Defenders must talk to each other, so they are aware of what is happening, where opponents are stationed, who is marking the ball, where the ball is being passed. Information obtained in this way will help the defensive team play as a team unit.

There are a number of different ways of organising a team to work as a team unit. Two of these methods will be briefly covered, these are sagging man to man defence and pressing man to man defence.

Sagging man to man defence

This is a defensive team tactic in which defenders marking opponents furthest from the ball move away from the attacking opponent towards the

70. Sagging man to man defence.

basket they are defending. This movement when a defender moves away from his opponent towards the basket he is defending is called sagging. A defender will also sag when he is marking an opponent who is outside a good shooting range. Figure 70 shows a sagging man to man defence. Each defender is responsible for one opponent but notice how each defender's position varies according to the opponent's position on court and the position of the ball. The defender under the basket marking player number 6 has sagged the most, and is giving the defence depth. If the attacking team passed the ball to the right hand side of the court the defender under the basket would move closer to number 6 and the defender marking the left forward number 7 would move under the basket. The attacking team will find it difficult to pass the ball to the under basket area when playing against a sagging defence and may be forced to take long shots.

94

71. Pressing man to man defence.

Pressing man to man defence

This is a man to man defence in which the defensive team attempt to force the opposing team into making some kind of error and thus lose possession of the ball. An important ingredient of a pressing defence is to mark the passing lanes and to prevent any of the attacking players from receiving the ball. In figure 71 a defensive team have adjusted their positions so that the passing lanes to each potential pass receiver is marked. The only attacking player that appears to be free to receive a pass is number 6, but the pass to this player will have to be high and long. This will give the defender time to move in for the interception.

95

72. (on following page) Action from Men's Cup Final.